The Demise of Our Nation and Our Family

*We Watch It, Read It, & Listen To It
Everyday*

By

Robert Knowles

Contents

PREFACE

I have lived through a lot of Presidents since being born over 60 years ago. Some considered good; some considered bad. However, in my lifetime, I have never seen a President scrutinized as our one we have in 2017. Every word he speaks he is humiliated and harassed by the news media and citizens. They are sometimes to the point of wanting to hurt him, slander, ridicule, insult, threaten to murder, threatened to rape our First Lady and his children also insulted and humiliated.

I would like to clarify; I do not identify with the Democratic Party, the Republican Party, the Independent Party or any other party. I am an American, and I vote for whom I feel is the best candidate, in any political race, whether it be City, County, School Board, State or National elections.I have never voted straight party, and my feeling on that it is that it is the biggest mistake in our elections today. There are good and bad on all sides, so let's try to get all of the good ones.

I am truly ashamed of the people of this country. I am ashamed of the ruthless, hating, cruel, citizens, politicians, Hollywood celebrities, and news media of this great Country that calls themselves Christians yet, have no morals. There are evil news reporters and talk show hosts who feel they have the right to purposely lie and report untruths that they do in the name of "anonymous sources, or "people close to" the situation, etc. and they call themselves "Journalist."

I realized long ago that three entities in our world have their agenda, The News Media, The Entertainment Business, and the Government, and that is to force people to believe what they want them to believe. They are trying to keep the focus on discrediting our President, Government, Politicians and our Religious beliefs to distract from the factual issues in our nation and the world.

When I grew up in the 50's and 60's, things were so much different than today. A Better different. Even while raising my children in the 70's 80' & 90's was pretty good. A lot of family time, doing things together, as a family. Today, in this electronic, digital world, the family unit has all but disappeared.

Most live their life with a cell phone attached to their hand and head, including our young children. As young as 5! Families don't pay attention to what is going on in the children's life or spouses, but what is happening on social media. People will say, that's not true my kids are involved in sports, dance, church, etc. But are they involved? When I go to these sporting events, parents are not focused on the game or event; they are focused on their cell phones. I've seen athletes at High School games texting on a cell phone from the sidelines. In church, people are more interested in their phones than in worship Go to a restaurant, and when you see a family, what are they doing? When I look, even while they are eating, they are on their phone, browsing, talking or texting. The parents have gotten to the point of using a cell phone as a babysitter, to keep them busy, so as the kids won't bother the parents.

These reasons are just the tip of the iceberg on why I'm writing this book. We need to take our children and our families back from the grip of social media, television and video games and the pure evil and perverseness of this world we live in today. I know some people won't agree with some of the things I say, but that's OK, we all have our opinions. Also, I may not agree with some, but I respect their right to express their thoughts and beliefs without gett angry or vindictive. All I hope is to make parents think about what is the best for their children, their marriage, and their family. Keep an open mind and let's hope we can help restore the family structure in America and the world. I am writing this in the hopes that it will shed some light on why this nation and our families is where it is and what the only way is that we can get out of this turmoil and turn this great country and our lives around.

This book is my opinion, my rant. I hope you enjoy.

CHAPTER 1

How We Got Here

God did not put us in the situation our country is in today, we have allowed it to happen ourselves. Only we can change it. And we can do this by following a few simple, yet very effective rules that have been handed down to us.

God gave us free will. We have the right to choose heaven or hell for ourselves and the success or failure of our great nation.

This country was founded on Christian and Biblical principles, and for centuries this country exploded in growth, wealth, happiness all while worshipping and praying to God. Towards the end of the 20th century and into the 21st, people have begun to ignore God; they are more in tune with social media, cell phones, vainness. We want to live out our lives online for everyone to see and judge. The internet and social media have ruined a lot of lives and careers by what has been posted about them and what they have posted. Journalism was once an honorable profession. But when the hunger for 24-hour news began, more stories were needed to fill the gaps, and thus began, the insiders, the unnamed sources, the anonymous sources and the people familiar with the situation.

We, The People, are being treated like naive children by the media; They are no better now than the supermarket tabloids.

Journalism's primary purpose is to hold power to account. This purpose has turned around. News writers talk show host, and bloggers work to enforce corporate media power, denouncing people and politicians who criticize their interests and bullying anyone that disagrees with its agenda. These media outlet owners have allowed governments occasionally to promote the interests of the poor, but never to hamper the interests of the rich. They also sought to discipline the rest of the media. The BBC, over the past 30 years, became a shadow of the gutsy broadcaster it was, and now treats big business with cringing deference because they have been bullied into following along with the rest of the world media. That is where the problem comes in. The media is now faced with President that will not follow the news media's agenda and is trying to do what he feels is best for our country but this does not meet with the corporate media's agenda. The same thing happened to Obama with the right-leaning media outlets.

Around 1914, Dean, Walter Williams, of the Missouri School of Journalism, wrote a code of ethics known as The Journalist's Creed. I will be surprised if even a small majority of journalists have ever heard of it let alone read it or strive to work with it in their daily profession, though it stands in bronze at the National Press Club in Washington, DC for all to see.

Here is what it states:

*1 *I believe in the profession of Journalism., I believe that the public journal is a public trust; that all connected with it are, to the full measure of responsibility, trustees for the public; that all acceptance of lesser service than the public service is a betrayal of this trust.*

- *I believe that clear thinking, clear statement, accuracy and fairness are fundamental to good journalism.*

- *I believe that a journalist should write only what he holds in his heart to be true.*

- *I believe that suppression of the news, for any consideration other than the welfare of society, is indefensible.*

- *I believe that no one should write as a journalist what he would not say as a gentleman; that bribery by one's own pocketbook is as much to be avoided as bribery by the pocketbook of another; that individual responsibility may not be escaped by pleading another's instructions or another's dividends.*

- *I believe that advertising, news and editorial columns should alike serve the best interests of readers; that a single standard of helpful truth and cleanness should prevail for all; that supreme test of good journalism is the measure of its public service.*

- *I believe that the journalism which succeeds the best-and best deserves success-fears God and honors man; is stoutly independent; unmoved by pride of opinion or greed of power; constructive, tolerant but never careless, self-controlled, patient, always respectful of its readers but always unafraid, is quickly indignant at injustice; is unswayed by the appeal of the privilege or the clamor of the mob; seeks to give every man a chance, and as far as law, an honest wage and recognition of human brotherhood can make it so, an equal chance; is profoundly patriotic while sincerely promoting international good will and cementing world-comradeship, is a journalism of humanity, of and for today's world.*

I see none of this being practiced in our daily news by any media outlet.

In the Bible, I think Peter best sums up the current day news media in 2 Peter 2:1-3: *"But false prophets also arose among the people, just as there will be false teachers among you, who will secretly bring in destructive heresies, even denying the Master who bought them, bringing upon themselves swift destruction. And many will follow their sensuality, and because of them, the way of truth will be blasphemed. And in their greed, they will exploit you with false words. Their condemnation from long ago is not idle, and their destruction is not asleep."*

It is incredible when I read through the Bible, and I come across prophecies that, when I read it, I think, "that is us today, right now!"

While researching for this book, I came across a report from 2010 on I-CNN blog post; it was posted by a housewife from Indiana with a screen name of venusstarlit;

"The Oath They Never Took" 2

"Truth indeed came once into the world with her divine Master, and was a perfect shape most glorious to look on:

15

*but when He ascended, and His apostles after Him were laid asleep, then straight arose a wicked race of deceivers, who ... took the virgin Truth, hewed her lovely form into a thousand pieces, and scattered them to the four winds."**

John Milton, in his Areopagitica, written over 340 years ago, seems to be preparing us for some disenchantment with the media.

Indeed, today there are complaints from all segments of society about news media incompetence, about over-hyping and trivializing the news, of strong and incessant ideological bias in the reporting of the news and even outright political propaganda being packaged and disseminated as the bona fide news of the day (and week).

This untenable track record has caused one reader to write: "It seems our news media needs a Hippocratic Oath more than our doctors do...." ("Post Needs Oath," by Mr. Gerald Rinell, Washington Inquirer, 1/18/85.)

Is it too much to ask, that journalists do something to show they're trying to do an honest job so we can trust them? After all, don't we pay for it in one way or another? Just ask the advertisers in your refrigerator, in your closet or your garage.

But, while not as "official" as an oath, nevertheless through the years there have been codes of ethics drawn up and endorsed by editors and journalists alike.

I sincerely wish the news business would once again recognize their obligation to their public and measure their performance by the standards they once enshrined--the oath they never took.

In her article "Are mainstream media prejudiced against God?" Denyse O'Leary, a Canadian author, said it well

"Due to waning public influence, traditional Western media increasingly promote government agendas. That

means tacitly accepting agendas that are sympathetic to government control of (accompanied, perhaps, by bailouts of) compliant media. For example, traditional media opposed and criticized "religion," but they do not risk criticizing Islam today. That just means they can't be where the action is or even honestly discuss what the action is (or at best, only half-heartedly, often long after new media are disseminating the news on Twitter, Facebook, blogzines, and blogs). Their biases end up making the most basic functions of news gathering impossible."

People say our current President is a terrible person! Who told us he is a terrible person? The media? How is he more terrible than others that came before him and 75% of our congrssional body today? I still go to President Reagans advice "Trust but verify." I have supported every President that has been elected no matter if I voted for them or not. I might not agree with their polices and beliefs, but they were and are our President. I learned a hard lesson 40 years ago when I went into the military. When I was going through my discharge process, a Captain reminded me " Once a Soldier, always a Soldier, remember your oath "!   And that oath is;

"I, ____, do solemnly swear (or affirm) that I will support and defend the Constitution of the United States against all enemies, foreign and domestic; that I will bear true faith and allegiance to the same; and that I will obey the orders of the President of the United States and the orders of the officers appointed over me, according to regulations and the Uniform Code of Military Justice. So help me God."

What this taught me is, we must always support our "Constitution and to bear true faith and allegiance to the same," no matter who the Commander in Chief is and no matter where we are in life. I believe " Once a soldier, always a soldier" because I am willing to defend our Constitution.

Chapter 2

Morality and Television

The morality of this world is at an all-time low and, yes, I feel social media, the news media, the internet, and television programming have a tremendous part of why this is happening.

Let's break each one of these down. We start with the last one first, Television and its programming. Today's programs are filled with things, like vulgar language, violence, sex, revenge and most with no morals.

The big rage as of this writing that comes immediately to mind is the shows about "real" housewives in different cities. When watching, two things pop into my mind. Why would anyone want to live in an atmosphere where "friends" are constantly arguing, screaming, and gossiping about each other? Is this what it is like to be rich? If so, I wouldn't want to be rich! All of the cast on these shows are in a very wealthy family. Of course, it's all scripted, and they are for the most part acting. It's fantasy

My solution? Get true real housewives that are working two jobs and trying to raise a family of 5 and are barely scraping by week to week? These women are the real life's drama in my mind, and it's not a fantasy. These are the women that don't need the notoriety, the glitz, and glamor. All they want is to raise their children in a stable, loving environment. Let's show them in their daily struggles of family life, and maybe it will share some idea's about how to raise a family. To me, these women are the stars in life, and all they ask in return is responsible children and God's blessing.

Then there is the Bachelor and Bachelorette shows. A new moral low in the life's relationships. So, a "Bachelor" gets to spend a week or two "courting" 4 or five young women to see who he wants to marry. He gets to spend a night with them in a secret room with no camera, and yes, it is widely reported, to have sex with them. I have read that one or two will always abstain, and good for them! And it's the same on the Bachelorette show, Just that the women get to court 5 or so men. So how can you make a moral decision in a couple of weeks, on TV, scripted, about who to spend the rest of your life with?

Would you want your daughter or son in this situation? One of the sad things is, the contestants don't get paid unless picked! Some quit their jobs and go into debt to be on the show.

My Solution? How about a reality show, nonscripted about a couple going through a year or so of dating, discovering and getting to know each other? This way would hopefully show some young people the right way to find the person you want to marry. This will give time for the couple to see things as they indeed are. Give time for that initial whirlwind of love settle down, let the dust clear and get the real picture.

Then there are these shows, several over the last few years about our government, especially the President of the United States. There is constant immoral relationships, adultery, murder, and corruption at every turn. I think people believe this is what it is honestly like (and maybe some of it is).

There are people in this world that cannot tell illusion or fantasy from the reality. It's called Psychosis. Psychosis is any form of severe mental disorder in which the individual's contact with reality becomes profoundly distorted.

Let 's look at these three, Illusion, Fantasy and Reality.

- An illusion is a false idea or belief, or a deceptive appearance or impression. An Illusion is what most of your television programs and movies are.

- A fantasy is an idea with no basis in reality and is your imagination of things that are improbable or impossible. Fantasy also is a lot of what we see in movies and TV; it's also called fiction.

- Reality is the state of things as they exist. Rather than as they may appear or might be imagined. Reality is what you can see, smell and feel so to say.

There are many options for television, without all of these types of programs. Angel TV, Glorystar, and Pureflix are just three of many that have children and family-friendly programming.

Chapter 3

The Internet

"It's got to be true, I saw it on the internet!" Yes, people still believe what they read on the internet is the truth, the whole truth, and nothing but the truth. Anytime someone has a question, and ache or pain, they "Google" it. Look up abdominal pain; Web MD says you may have indigestion, constipation, a stomach virus, or if you're a woman, menstrual cramps. Irritable bowel syndrome (IBS)Crohn's disease, Food poisoning, Food allergies, Gas. You may also get abdominal pain if you're lactose intolerant or have ulcers or pelvic inflammatory disease. Some other causes include Hernia, Gallstones, Kidney stones, Endometriosis, Gastroesophageal reflux disease (GERD)or Appendicitis. "Wow. How about if the pain lasts a few days and Pepto Bismol or Milk of Magnesia doesn't help, go to the doctor. Don't fill your head with every probable cause or disease that will cause stress in most people and even make things worse. Go to your Doctor!

This brings me right back to our three friends, Illusion, Fantasy, and Reality. Things you read on the internet are in these three categories, and it is sometimes tough to tell the difference, even if you don't have psychosis.

We have everything from miracle cures, to get rich schemes to the daily news. Almost anything you can think of in your mind is on the internet, how to make bombs, how to disappear, and how to steal other people's identity. It's all there. But, is it all necessary.

There have been many business and personal reputations ruined because of the internet. When you make an enemy, for whatever reason or how big or small it is, people can rally the troops and post continuous negative things about your business, yourself, and your family and friends. It happens every day. Look at all of the sex abuse scandals, corruption claims and physical abuse claims every day, some true, others unfounded, but once they are made public, game over. The internet will try and sentence you and your reputation.

I believe that the internet has also diluted the truth in our news reporting. There are so many self-proclaimed journalists and so-called new agencies on the internet now; it's impossible to know what the truth is, and no, Snopes is not the answer. It is loaded with bias "fact-checking." So are sites like the Daily Caller, and Factcheck.org. I always first look at the publisher. Usually, they are already known for having a left or right leaning agenda. The easiest way to fact check on your own, is, for example, if a House or Senate bill is in the debate stage, to learn the facts, go and read the proposed legislation for yourself. Don't take other peoples opinion as fact! Misinformation is what starts so many misunderstandings and mistrust in our daily lives.

When the news media, newspapers, talk shows and television news know they will be fact-checked on items they report on; they will claim it now as an" Analysis." Their response is, "it's not a lie or misinformation, that is how I analyzed it," knowing that that is not how the majority of-of people will perceive it. These people take it as the truth.

There are also many good things about the internet. There is a lot of useful information, from Dictionaries, Thearasus, Encyclopedias, Bibles, Online Education and even recipes and cooking lessons. So, it's not all bad. In fact, I feel there is more good than bad on the internet.

My Solution? I think that the internet must be controlled, to an extent. There are so many people getting swindled out of money buying useless products, it is criminal. It's the old snake oil salesman on steroids! I believe a business like this should be vetted before allowing to push off these products on unsuspected people. I'm not sure or smart enough to know how to do this, but some people can, I'm sure. These sites must be vetted well before you allow your children to use them. The internet is an electronic library and should operate like one.

CHAPTER 4

Hate, Opinion, and Negativity in Today's News

When you turn on the evening news, no matter the channel or pick up a daily paper, the first thing you see or hear is negativity. The reason is the media wants you to get angry immediately so that they can feed you more hate, misconceptions, and sometimes unverified facts. The Government doesn't run our country any longer, the news media does. They control so many of our lawmakers, on both sides of the aisle, they will do anything the news media wants as long as it helps the lawmaker's agendas, no matter if it is true or not. The ones that haven't gone along have paid the price. The media will leak information about lawmakers, like information about mistresses, lobbyist payoff, bad debt, etc., this keeps the others in line, not wanting their good names smeared. Not all politicians are bad apples. We have some very good Democrat, Republicans, and

Independents that are sincerely interested in what is best for the citizens, but much more that are not. Their only interest is keeping the special interest happy, so when election time comes, they know the money will flow.

The more attention that the news media can report on the negativity in our government executive branch over what the President has said, not said, about Russia, about this that or the other. They, the media, want us to believe that the President is getting nothing done. I was beginning to think that way when I again thought, "trust but verify." I verified, and now I know the truth. Our current President I feel is running what is being called the shadow government. These behind the scenes activities has accomplished quite a bit. The President is busy distracting the media. This lets his people get the work done with little pressure from the media. Wether you are Republican, Democrat, or whomever; it will pay for you to verify what you read. The media loves to point out how he has not lived up to his promises. That is another way they spread propaganda. He has four years to accomplish his agenda. He has been in office a little over 200 days and had not had the support of our lawmakers because of their fear of how the news media will smear them if they do support him. Trump is pretty slick at keeping the media and Democrats distracted, while his administration gets things done.

That is why you never hear the mainstream media reporting positive things about the government in our country. They want you to think that there is nothing positive and make you believe it is the Presidents fault.

Do yourself a favor, again, verify, what the news media reports. It's not always factual.

I saw a comment in the media a few days ago that said the person driving the car in the

the Charlottesville incident could not get a fair trial because Trump called him a murderer.

What? The news media is telling me he can't get a fair trial with all of the news media bias, opinion, and biography on the person? They have already tried him on national television. More things the media want you to believe. Everything is our Presidents fault. Again, just use common sense logic, something the news media hope you don't use.

Have you ever noticed when the media are reporting on a terrible incident where several people have lost their lives? Every outlet has a different count on how many are dead and injured?

The reason? They have not checked the facts, and they are just "shooting from the hip" trying to get the scoop, true or not, they know if one news outlet reports ten dead and if they report fifteen, more people will read their story about the 15. Their thought is we'll retract it later, maybe.

I have found I don't watch the news any longer to get the news; I watch it to analyze it, research and get to the truth. All mainstream media, ABC, NBC, CBS FOX, CNN, MSNBC, & CNBC and others give their opinions. They all violate the sacred code of Journalism we talked about in chapter one. The media has disrupted our justice system to the point of no one in this country can get a fair trial. The media loves to hold trial against individuals on television, social media, and print. They love bringing in so-called experts to give their opinion on why that person did what they did, the day of and after the crime. Whatever happened to innocent until proven guilty? Let the courts do their job.

I see people always saying our Government is a joke across the world. Who has made it the joke? I think the media has by the way they report the news. It's always negative always on the attack of our government. They become upset when they are not given information on national defense issues like in Iraq, North Korea, Afghanistan, etc.

They feel they have a right t this information, but I disagree. Our news media would report it and put our and our ally's troops at risk. But do they care? No, they don't. Just in the last few days, the President announced that more troops would be going to Afghanistan. Th media, of course, want to know how many, when and for how long. They use the excuse that they need to know because parents want to know how many more of our kids are going to war. I feel they want the enemy to know so they can have more negative news about the failure of our government. The media is constantly feeding our enemies with information. They love reporting on our "aging" fleet in the Navy, or under-equipped soldiers. They want our enemies to know our countries weaknesses. Why would anyone do this or even want to do this? Oh, I forgot, the scoop is more important than our country or human life. The media continues to prove this when classified information was leaked, instead of doing the honorable thing and reporting it to the authorities, for the sake of the scoop, they reported it to the world. Some may argue that it wasn't harmful information, but that's not the issue. The issue is they did it and should pay for it criminally. What if the next leak is about military operations?

Foreign terrorist groups are not worried about attacking America. American is destroying itself from the inside, by the media, its politicians, and its gullible citizens. They can sit back and wait until the time is right and just waltz in.

So the big news recently is, of course, the removing statues of all Confederate figures. They are offensive people say. Why is now they are offensive after most have been in place for well over 100 years? Why now? Why tear them down, put them in a museum, it's part of our history. I read today, people in New York want Christopher Columbus's statue removed because he was a slave owner! So who's next? Washington, Jefferson, Grant, William Penn? The statues honoring some Texas heroes of Texas history, like

Sam Houston and William Travis? I'm sure most religious statues will go before then, the ten commandments already have.

So many today are living in the past about racism and slavery, picking the scab of a past wound and they won't let it heal. Thanks to the news media. There are problems with slavery in our nation today that if all the energy spent in the past would be used for today's issues, we could eradicate slavery that is ongoing in the United States today. Hundreds of Mexican citizens, South Americans and Chinese risk their lives every day to come to our country, and most end up either dead in the back of a cargo truck, in a container on a ship, out in the desert or become slaves to the sex and drug market or farm and construction labor. They are being sold by their countrymen into slavery, just as the slaves from Africa were in the 17 and 1800's, all in the name of greed. There are hundreds of thousands of refugees that try to come to America to escape the atrocities they face, but end up being taken advantage of when they do arrive. Many of these refugees are also trapped in a slavery lifestyle, in the restaurant industries, construction, and terrible underground drug and sex slaves. I pray our Nation will wake up and address the slave trade that ongoing today and leave history as history. Sanctuary cities are bad; bad because these slaves are trapped in a world where with the political corruption, they are doomed. My prayer is we can end current day slavery so that this country does not have another period that we did in the past. We can't change the past, but we can change today and the future. History, my friends, is beginning to repeat itself, just a different race.

I believe the most one-sided, racist, hate-filled, bigoted talk show is the View. Who's view? It's always theirs. If you disagree with the host's view, they slam you, talk about you with pure hateful dialogue, argue that they are right and of course, they post terrible things about you on twitter and facebook, that is right after they cite scripture and call themselves Christian. If only they truly understood what they say about scripture, the true meaning of what they are saying.

There are still reporters out there that are real Journalist, they follow the creed and are honorable people. Most work for the small local papers. They report the facts and let the reader form their own opinion. They are far, and few between though, and are not respected in the mainstream media because they won't follow the status quo.

In a nutshell, I believe that the news media are the instigators of hate, racism, bigotry and they are most responsible for dividing our nation. They are doing it for their hunger for news; The media uses fear tactics on people who state opinions, not in line with the press. I believe their feeling is that if there is no news, make the news. Politicians and special interest groups use the media as an attack dog.

CHAPTER 5

Television, Movies and Social Media

Most entertainers in our nation are starved for attention, out of work actors and actresses that feed off of fame, and money; they will go along with whatever they think is popular at the time. They will make hateful and lewd statements about our politicians, our flag, our Constitution and of course the Bible. It sickens me to hear an entertainer tell how much of a Christian they are and then go onto speak hatefully about people that they disagree with or that disagree with them. This behavior is more evident with talk show host. They have an agenda that they want on push on their show, which is mostly hateful and unsubstantiated claims about people. I refer to these talk shows as tabloids on TV. No matter who they represent or political party they identify with, they spread gossip, untruths, and hearsay. They rarely seem to verify the "facts" that they spew out on their show. These hosts claim it is their opinion, but God helps you if your opinion doesn't align with theirs. Of course, you will even hear during some of these topics; they talk about how things are against their Christian upbringing! You mean like gossip, lies, and hate?

Attention and money, it's only their opinion that counts, no one else. The old saying, if someone says the sky is blue, they would disagree. That's when the show's producer will through up the sign that reads "loud applause."It's all scripted, all just a big game. They want you to believe that the audience is in total agreement with what they believe.

Most actors and actresses today have their agenda's also, and with that fame, use it to push that they want to push that agenda. Some are good, like breast cancer PSA's and fundraisers, drug rehabilitation announcements, and alcohol and drug PSA's. But there are the ones that that push an agenda of hate and racism and the murder of our

President, oh, and some of these claim to be "Christians." At State Legislator in Missouri stated she wished Trump would be assassinated, then tried to apologize and talked about how much of a Christian she was, etc. If she were a true Christian, she would have never said it or even thought of it in the first place.

We must always remember, they are actors, they act, they pretend. That's their life, their profession. If something is being protested or debated and the actors think they can cash in on the moment, using their fame and "acting" like they are sincere, they will do it. This will, they hope, build their fan base. Not all actors fall into this category, there are still honorable women and men that work in the profession, by keeping their lives private and personal.

Next is our pro sports entertainers. Yes, they are entertainers. They are very skilled, athletic and smart entertainers. They have a gift that we all wished for when we were children. Be it baseball, football, basketball, soccer or any other sport, most all of us had that dream. For a lot of pro sports figures that dream turns into a nightmare. First, there is the money, the greed, lust for fame, sex and the drugs. This combination has ruined many lives of professional athletes. There are the few in the professional that is sincere and remain great role models for our children. These athletes remember growing up and working hard to accomplish their goals and knew what to stay away from to get where they wanted to be, and they are thankful. Then there are ones that, with their fame, have their agenda to push, usually though, like movie actors, they will follow what popular in the hope of widening their fan base. This type of agenda usually backfires on most. They have no morals and portray conceit, bitterness and hate towards others because of their problems in life. They need someone to blame, for where they are in life. Their professional career is heading downhill, and they want that last minute of recognition and fame, no matter what it is related to.

So, money and fame is the main divisor here, and the worship of it. Some athletes feel money will solve all of their problems, but usually, it just causes more.

Chapter 6

Our Dysfunction Government

Our Government has been dysfunctional for years. Our lawmakers have reached the point of not caring about the citizens, but only about themselves and their special interest. Citizens only vote, special interest have money, and in our legislator's world, money trumps citizens any day of the week. I may be a little gentle here, but some call it corruption.

Our lawmakers are mostly millionaires and lawyers who seek to make that great living, with a salary for life, automatic raises that they can vote on for themselves, healthcare for their lifetime and so many other perks. One thing they love is they don't have to be accountable to their constituents, only to the special interest and the news media. Give a Senator, or Congressperson a hot topic controversy, like the President, said "and" when they thought he should have said, " or." That is what the people we have elected to make and uphold our laws are doing. It is obvious, but no one calls them out. If they do, they are subject to attacks by the media that will ruin their lives. That's most probably what will happen to me when this book gets published!

I must touch on our lawmaker's inability and unwillingness to uphold the law of the land. Illegal immigration. It's illegal, against a federal law that our lawmakers passed years ago. It's on the books, why won't they enforce it? Simple, they need the money. The money pumped into elections from the special interest that support these illegals, and they need the votes, yes, illegals vote. Some have been caught, but the majority get away with it. It is hard to catch them when you can't ask for an ID.

That brings me back to sanctuary cities. Local government and law enforcement say that illegal immigration is a Federal law and the local police do not have the resources to do anything. They are also afraid that if the capture illegals, other illegals won't report the crime.

What about other Federal Laws, bank robbery, and kidnapping, just naming a couple. Are our local governments going to overlook these crimes also? A law is a law, and crime is a crime. We pay our government officials to enforce our laws and prevent crime and prosecute criminals. So how can they be allowed to pick and choose what laws to enforce?

I'm not going to defend President Trump granting Sheriff Joe Arapo a pardon, but what I do question is our Federal Government punishing a law enforcement official for upholding the Federal law. I can't explain it. All I can say it all stinks of corruption. The media saying the pardon undermines our judicial system, I counter with charging the Sheriff for doing his job is a miscarriage of justice. It was always claimed it was profiling he was charged with. Common sense would tell anyone that most of the illegals are Mexican, so why look for a black person or a white person when 95% of illegals that cross the border are Mexican or South American? When a crime is committed, and the person is described as a tall white female, is it profiling when the police stop all tall white women?

One thing that has stuck in my mind about how corrupt and delusional our lawmakers are is when Nancy Pelosi was debating the affordable care act, and she said:" don't worry about whats in it, vote for it, then we will read it." This is our lawmakers in action, not a care in the world about the citizens of this country, and they question President Trump's stability? There are so many lawmakers on all sides, that when I listen to an interview or their rants, I'm very concerned that these people represent us? They don't know who the President is; they have no idea what countries we are aiding in war efforts, they don't care. My thought on this is, most people are required drug and alcohol testing before that can get a job and are subject to random tests after. I would love for this to be a requirement for all elected officials who represent us in Federal, State or Local Government.

DACA

Well, President Trump, rescinded DACA today. I agree in theory with the program and am very happy these young dreamers can take advantage of the program. However, it is very flawed, and these young people were set up for what is happening now. On June 15, 2012, President Obama created a new policy calling for deferred action for certain undocumented young people who came to the U.S. as children. Applications under the program which is called Deferred Action for Childhood Arrivals ("DACA") began on August 15, 2012. That is the sad thing; it's policy when it needs to be part of the immigration law, which only our lazy lawmakers can do. All President Trump did is rescind something that the last President should not have done. If Obama wanted DACA, he should have done it the right way. It is the job of the lawmakers to do this, not the President. President Obama had an expiration of three years put on every approved applicant .Remember; these are undocumented Aliens. They are not citizens. I feel sorry for them because Obama did this to them without giving them a pathway to citizenship, they have been in Limbo for five years. Every three years they have to request a renewal, and risk not getting it. So now, let's see if our do-nothing lawmakers can get this done for the sake of these dreamers. There is a right way to do things, so now let's see if they will get it done the right way. President Trump is trying to do it the right way and give the well deserving dreamers a true path to citizenship, not a piece of paper that expires every three years. The U.S. immigration law offers very few options to go from being an illegal or undocumented immigrant to a U.S. permanent resident (with a green card). DACA is not a permanent residency. According It is an exercise of discretion by immigration services granting temporary legal presence and work authorization in the United States. Since DACA is not an immigrant visa, there is no option to directly adjust from a DACA status into Legal Permanent Residency (LPR) / Green Card. All Trump has done is forcing our lawmakers to act and get this into the Immigration law and give them that path. It's not as easy to change the law as policy is, and just was, to change. I am for DACA, but with a path to citizenship, and that is all President Trump has done, he's trying to get Congress to come up with that solution, after all, it is their job.

HARVEY

In the middle of starting this writing, Hurricane Harvey decided to pay a visit to my area, Houston. With a lot of preparations, my wife, two mini – schnauzers and I hunkered down. We live about 15 miles due west of the city limits, and our neighborhood spared the flooding. However, the horror was unfolding before our eyes, right on live TV. People being rescued, rescuing themselves, and begging for help from rooftops. There is one rescue that will stick out in my mind forever. A lady is shown struggling in water that is rushing across I-10, you can see a truck upside down in the water near her. The water is so fast that rescuers can't get to her, we are on the edge of our seats praying and shouting at the TV for her to hang on. Finally, a boat made it to her in what appeared to be in the nick of time! But then, the unthinkable happened, She stood up on the side of the boat and jumped right back into the water! We sat there in utter shock. She was finally rescued again and brought to a hospital for evaluation. I thought about why someone would do this, why when you are rescued, go right back into the danger? Was she suicidal, in shock? Who knows, but I did and still do pray for her recovery. While trying to rationalize this behavior, I thought, this sounds just like our nation! Always jumping right back into bad things we just got out of.

During the evacuations, you have never seen so many people coming together, all races, nationalities, and religions. It didn't matter; people knew what was right and they knew they had to act and act they did. I am so proud of Houston and all of Texas for the way everyone pulled together, but then, there is the national news media. They have to find something negative. First, it was trying to get people to blame the great mayor of Houston for not being prepared. Sorry folks, we live here, we say first hand the action of city and county governments that were working to get like well-oiled machines, a few bumps here and there, but all in all, I am proud of the job all of these leaders have done.

Well, the blame game didn't work, so now the focus is on our President, just hoping he will mess up. The media are, as usual, scrutinizing every word he says. They don't care about the people that have been devastated; they are trying to figure out how to blame the slightest misstep by the government in aid efforts. No good there either, so the next step was to make fun of the First Lady's high heel shoes as she was leaving Washington! The journalist has stooped so low, that they would rather find fault with anything they can make our government and government officials look bad. They don't care about anything else, except the media's special interest.

I saw a CNN reporter interviewing Gov. Abbot. She didn't ask how things were going, what the State needed, her first question was, " Are you happy with

President Trump's response to the hurricane? " You could see that the question immensely irritated the Governor.

Most news media doesn't care, all they want, as I have said time and time again, is to find a way to discredit and smear the current Administration, on the City, State, and Federal level, whoever it is. I feel, and it should be apparent, they are doing this for the big money advertisers and special interest. The media has always been good at destroying people that do not follow their agenda. I may be next, but that's OK, I'm a Christian, and the media has been persecuting Christians as a whole for a long time now, I'm used to it and am well able to defend my faith and myself.

To end this chapter, I would like to thank all Texans, (yes the football team also,) all of the other States that helped Texas in this terrible disaster, and continue to help. I would like to give special thanks to the Cajun

Navy, who gave their own time to risk their lives to save their neighbors, Jim "Mattress Mack" McIngvale, Mr. Houston, Who is always helping Houston, and we can't forget J.J. Watt, he raised Twenty-Seven million dollars! Thank You!

To the mayors, county judges and emergency officials of all the cities in and surrounding Houston, thank you. It was a tough and thankless job, but you stuck with it and you stuck with us.

And Finally, thanks to all the officials in the Corpus Christi, Port Aransas, Beaumont, Port Arthur, Lumberton, Silsbee, Texas and Lake Charles, Louisiana. It was a surprise to every one of the devastation your citizens suffered, the news media ignored most of you, but all of Texas was and still is with you.

Chapter 7

Violence in America

I hear a lot about mental illness is the reason for school shootings, which I do firmly believe but I have not seen anything mentioned about poor or bad parenting, which can cause mental illness. Look back at the most violent murders in prison, and most talks about they were miserable and abusive childhood, they were beaten, sexually abused and where their parents were never involved in their lives. Then there's "peer upbringing? That is what most gangs are. When the family rejects their children, they hunger for attention, acceptance, and love. And gangs offer that to them., and they will do anything to get the praise and stay in the good graces of gang leaders.

People can protest for or against guns, that is their right. I have defended and will still defend that right, that is a right that they have because guns afforded them that right. Protest never solve the problem. I believe in responsible gun ownership, I believe in the second amendment. I was in the military and used a gun, I was a police officer and used a gun, and I have had to defend my family and my home, with a gun. All I ask is that people that are protesting and wanting change on gun laws, educate yourself on the guns, the difference in an assault rifle and hunting rifles. Remember, the definition of "Assault "is "make a physical attack on." Any gun can be used as an assault weapon. Learn about the constitution, the second Amendment and WHY it was written.

We must pressure our elected officials and demand the changes that are being sought. However, remember, elected officials don't answer to you, the voter, they answer to the lobbyist. That is where the focus needs to be. Why should we allow paid lobbyist? They get paid to sway a politician's stance on issues that the backers of the lobbyist want. Many organizations such a Pharmaceutical, Gun, Environmental, Oil & Gas, Chemical and so many more pay lobbyists to get politicians to see things their way. It's a legal way to corruption. Doing away with lobbyist and special interest contributions, the politicians will start listening to the voters.

Can God Save America? Sure, he can, but will he? Why should he?

God did not put us in the situation our country is in today, we have allowed it to happen ourselves. Only we can change it. And we can do this by following a few simple, yet very effective rules that have been handed down to us.

God gave us free will. We have the right to choose heaven or hell for ourselves and the success or failure of our great nation and ours and our families.

In his song entitled "Do Something" Christian music artist Matthew West ask God to do something about the way the world has become, and Gods answer to his prayer was "I have, I sent you." God has given us the ability to change and to change the ways of this country and the world.

Jesus came to do the will of God. [34] Jesus said to them, "My food is to do the will of Him who sent Me and to finish His work. John 4:34

We cannot resist the will of God. " Who can resist the love of God? What God wills to be done, must be done. He wills the salvation of all men because it is part of His love. God cannot tolerate continuous sin, hatred, and rebellion against Him. If he wills the salvation of all humans, He wills all humans to be saved; it shall be accomplished.

John 12:44-50 New King James Version (NKJV)

44 Then Jesus cried out and said, "He who believes in Me, believes not in Me but in Him who sent Me. **45** And he who sees Me sees Him who sent Me. **46** I have come *as* a light into the world, that whoever believes in Me should not abide in darkness. **47** And if anyone hears My words and does not [a]believe, I do not judge him; for I did not come to judge the world but to save the world. **48** He who rejects Me, and does not receive My words, has that which judges him—the word that I have spoken will judge him in the last day. **49** For I have not spoken on My own *authority;* but the Father who sent Me gave Me a command, what I should say and what I should speak. **50** And I know that His command is everlasting life. Therefore, whatever I speak, just as the Father has told Me, so I speak."

Chapter 8

The Guide to Save Ourselves, Our Family and our World

When I here someone that life didn't come with and instruction manual, I must disagree. Some will say that it's the Bible. However, it more specific, it's the Book of Exodus Chapter 20, its known as The Ten Commandments.

The Ten Commandments; Exodus 20: 1-17

20 And God spoke all these words, saying:

[2] "I *am* the LORD your God, who brought you out of the land of Egypt, out of the house of [a]bondage.

[3] "You shall have no other gods before Me.

[4] "You shall not make for yourself a carved image—any likeness *of anything* that *is* in heaven above, or that *is* in the earth beneath, or that *is* in the water under the earth; [5] you

shall not bow down to them nor [b]serve them. For I, the LORD your God, *am* a jealous God, visiting[c] the iniquity of the fathers upon the children to the third and fourth *generations* of those who hate Me, [6] but showing mercy to thousands, to those who love Me and keep My commandments.

[7] "You shall not take the name of the LORD your God in vain, for the LORD will not hold *him* guiltless who takes His name in vain.

[8] "Remember the Sabbath day, to keep it holy. [9] Six days you shall labor and do all your work, [10] but the seventh day *is* the Sabbath of the LORD your God. *In it* you shall do no work: you, nor your son, nor your daughter, nor your male servant, nor your female servant, nor your cattle, nor your stranger who *is* within your gates. [11] For *in* six days the LORD made the heavens and the earth, the sea, and all that

is in them, and rested the seventh day. Therefore, the LORD blessed the Sabbath day and hallowed it.

[12] "Honor your father and your mother, that your days may be long upon the land which the LORD your God is giving you.

[13] "You shall not murder.

[14] "You shall not commit adultery.

[15] "You shall not steal.

[16] "You shall not bear false witness against your neighbor.

[17] "You shall not covet your neighbor's house; you shall not covet your neighbor's wife, nor his male servant, nor his female servant, nor his ox, nor his donkey, nor anything that *is* your neighbor's."

We can be saved, and God can save us, but it's up to us make it happen. It is the will of God that all humans be saved. God inspires the hearts of the good to pray for the salvation of all men, and say, as Jesus said, "Your kingdom come. Your will be done on earth as it is in heaven. "Matt. 6:10.

Pick up the Bible, read it, learn to understand it. It is our manual for our life. Use it, your life depends on it.

END

NOTES

*All Scripture taken from the New King James Version®.

Copyright © 1982 by Thomas Nelson.

Page 7 *1 -The Journalist's Creed | The Long Version.

(n.d.). Retrieved from

https://longversion.wordpress.com/2012/09/23/the-

journalists-creed/

Page 9 -* 2The Oath They Never Took | Renaissance man's

Blog. (n.d.). Retrieved from

https://renaissancemansblog.wordpress.com/the-oath-they-

never-took/